THE ONE-MINUTE GRATITUDE JOURNAL FOR TEENS

SIMPLE JOURNAL TO INCREASE GRATITUDE AND HAPPINESS

This Journal belongs to:

_____

ISBN: 978-1-952358-22-7

Gratitude

Gratitude is a feeling of appreciation for what one has. It is a feeling of thankfulness for the blessings we have received. Cultivating an attitude of gratitude yields many benefits: physical, mental and spiritual. Feeling gratitude in the present moment makes you happier and more relaxed, and improves your overall health and well-being.

With an eye made quiet by the power of harmony, and the deep power of joy,
we see into the life of things.
~ William Wordsworth

Gratitude doesn't just have to be about the big things. It can also be for small, everyday events. You can be thankful for simple things such as enjoying a movie or just talking to an old friend for the first time in a long while. There is always something that you can be grateful for in your life. It is all about appreciating the things around you rather than taking them all for granted.

Write down three to four things that you are grateful for each day. You will not only feel good as you write them down, but you will experience gratitude during the day as well. A person experiencing gratitude feels a sense of joy and abundance in their life. They also feel more connected with other people and have increased energy.

Gratitude should always be expressed in the present tense and is more powerful when combined with the perceived benefit so that an emotional connection is made. Instead of writing, *"I am grateful for my health and well-being,"* it is better to write, *"I am grateful for my health and well-being and it makes me feel great."*

No duty is more urgent than that of returning thanks.
~ James Allen

One of the healthiest and most positive things we can do in our lives is to express our gratitude to the people around us. Tell someone how much you appreciate them. Tell someone that something they did mattered to you. When people make an impact, let them know. We are usually too quick to point out people's faults and ways in which they have wronged us, while slow to bestow recognition for good deeds and favors.

If someone makes you feel good, make them feel good too. By expressing our gratitude to others, we are making the world a better place and encouraging the things that we want to see more of. Say, *"Thank you."* Make a difference. Seek out the best in people and when you find it, say something about it.

A gentle word, a kind look, a good-natured smile can work wonders and accomplish miracles.
~ William Hazlitt

Learn something new every day. This is a process to simply learn and expand your life. In this journal, write down something new you have learned today.

Write down something amazing that happened in this journal every day. More amazing things will come into your life when you notice these and are appreciative for them.

There are pages in this journal where you can just draw something. If you don't feel like drawing anything, simply paste a beautiful picture onto this page. Our minds react better to imagery and this is a great way to feel gratitude and appreciation.

Gratitude makes us more optimistic and compassionate. True happiness lies within us. By keeping a record of your gratitude in a journal, you will store positive energy, gain clarity in your life, and have greater control of your thoughts and emotions.

Each day, write down three to four things that you are grateful for in this journal and turn your ordinary moments into blessings.

It is never too late to be what you might have been.

~ George Eliot

Happiness depends upon ourselves.
— Aristotle

Day: _____   Date: __/__/___

1. Today I am *Grateful* for:

_____

_____

_____

_____

2. Today I learned...

_____

3. Something amazing that happened today:

_____

Day: _____   Date: __/__/___

1. Today I am *Grateful* for:

_____

_____

_____

_____

2. Today I learned...

_____

3. Something amazing that happened today:

_____

Day: _____   Date: __/__/___

1. Today I am *Grateful* for:

_____

_____

_____

_____

2. Today I learned...

_____

3. Something amazing that happened today:

_____

Happiness resides not in possessions, and not in gold,
happiness dwells in the soul. — Democritus

Day: _____   Date: __/__/___

1. Today I am *Grateful* for:

_____

_____

_____

_____

2. Today I learned...

_____

3. Something amazing that happened today:

_____

Day: _____   Date: __/__/___

1. Today I am *Grateful* for:

_____

_____

_____

_____

2. Today I learned...

_____

3. Something amazing that happened today:

_____

Day: _____   Date: __/__/___

1. Today I am *Grateful* for:

_____

_____

_____

_____

2. Today I learned...

_____

3. Something amazing that happened today:

_____

Cheerfulness is the best promoter of health and is as friendly
to the mind as to the body. — Joseph Addison

Day: _____   Date: __/__/___

1. Today I am *Grateful* for:

_____

_____

_____

_____

2. Today I learned...

_____

3. Something amazing that happened today:

_____

Day: _____   Date: __/__/___

1. Today I am *Grateful* for:

_____

_____

_____

_____

2. Today I learned...

_____

3. Something amazing that happened today:

_____

Day: _____   Date: __/__/___

1. Today I am *Grateful* for:

_____

_____

_____

_____

2. Today I learned...

_____

3. Something amazing that happened today:

_____

The sun does not shine for a few trees and flowers,
but for the wide world's joy. — Henry Ward Beecher

Day: _____   Date: __/__/___

1. Today I am *Grateful* for:
_____
_____
_____
_____

2. Today I learned...
_____

3. Something amazing that happened today:
_____

Day: _____   Date: __/__/___

1. Today I am *Grateful* for:
_____
_____
_____
_____

2. Today I learned...
_____

3. Something amazing that happened today:
_____

Day: _____   Date: __/__/___

1. Today I am *Grateful* for:
_____
_____
_____
_____

2. Today I learned...
_____

3. Something amazing that happened today:
_____

It is not knowledge, but the act of learning, not possession but the act of getting there, which grants the greatest enjoyment.
— Carl Friedrich

Day: _____   Date: __/__/___

1. Today I am *Grateful* for:

_____

_____

_____

_____

2. Today I learned...

_____

3. Something amazing that happened today:

_____

Day: _____   Date: __/__/___

1. Today I am *Grateful* for:

_____

_____

_____

_____

2. Today I learned...

_____

3. Something amazing that happened today:

_____

Day: _____   Date: __/__/___

1. Today I am *Grateful* for:

_____

_____

_____

_____

2. Today I learned...

_____

3. Something amazing that happened today:

_____

Day: _____   Date: __/__/____

1. Today I am *Grateful* for:

_____
_____
_____
_____

2. Today I learned...

_____

3. Something amazing that happened today:

_____

Day: _____   Date: __/__/____

1. Today I am *Grateful* for:

_____
_____
_____
_____

2. Today I learned...

_____

3. Something amazing that happened today:

_____

Day: _____   Date: __/__/____

1. Today I am *Grateful* for:

_____
_____
_____
_____

2. Today I learned...

_____

3. Something amazing that happened today:

_____

When unhappy, one doubts everything; when happy,
one doubts nothing. — Joseph Roux

Day: _____   Date: _/_/___

1. Today I am *Grateful* for:

_____

_____

_____

_____

2. Today I learned...

_____

3. Something amazing that happened today:

_____

Day: _____   Date: _/_/___

1. Today I am *Grateful* for:

_____

_____

_____

_____

2. Today I learned...

_____

3. Something amazing that happened today:

_____

Day: _____   Date: _/_/___

1. Today I am *Grateful* for:

_____

_____

_____

_____

2. Today I learned...

_____

3. Something amazing that happened today:

_____

Find ecstasy in life; the mere sense of living is joy enough.
— Emily Dickinson

Day: _____   Date: __/__/___

1. Today I am *Grateful* for:

_____

_____

_____

_____

2. Today I learned...

_____

3. Something amazing that happened today:

_____

Day: _____   Date: __/__/___

1. Today I am *Grateful* for:

_____

_____

_____

_____

2. Today I learned...

_____

3. Something amazing that happened today:

_____

Day: _____   Date: __/__/___

1. Today I am *Grateful* for:

_____

_____

_____

_____

2. Today I learned...

_____

3. Something amazing that happened today:

_____

Do not mind anything that anyone tells you about anyone else.
Judge everyone and everything for yourself. — Henry James

Day: _____   Date: _/_/___

1. Today I am *Grateful* for:

_____

_____

_____

_____

2. Today I learned...

_____

3. Something amazing that happened today:

_____

Day: _____   Date: _/_/___

1. Today I am *Grateful* for:

_____

_____

_____

_____

2. Today I learned...

_____

3. Something amazing that happened today:

_____

Day: _____   Date: _/_/___

1. Today I am *Grateful* for:

_____

_____

_____

_____

2. Today I learned...

_____

3. Something amazing that happened today:

_____

Draw something

Events will take their course, it is no good of being angry at them;
he is happiest who wisely turns them to the best account.
— Euripides

Day: _____   Date: __/__/___

1. Today I am *Grateful* for:

_____

_____

_____

_____

2. Today I learned...

_____

3. Something amazing that happened today:

_____

Day: _____   Date: __/__/___

1. Today I am *Grateful* for:

_____

_____

_____

_____

2. Today I learned...

_____

3. Something amazing that happened today:

_____

Day: _____   Date: __/__/___

1. Today I am *Grateful* for:

_____

_____

_____

2. Today I learned...

_____

3. Something amazing that happened today:

_____

Live your life as though your every act were to become
a universal law. — Immanuel Kant

Day: _____   Date: __/__/____

1. Today I am *Grateful* for:

_____

_____

_____

_____

2. Today I learned...

_____

3. Something amazing that happened today:

_____

Day: _____   Date: __/__/____

1. Today I am *Grateful* for:

_____

_____

_____

_____

2. Today I learned...

_____

3. Something amazing that happened today:

_____

Day: _____   Date: __/__/____

1. Today I am *Grateful* for:

_____

_____

_____

_____

2. Today I learned...

_____

3. Something amazing that happened today:

_____

Three grand essentials to happiness in this life are something to do, something to love, and something to hope for.
— Joseph Addison

Day: _____   Date: __/__/____

1. Today I am *Grateful* for:

_____

_____

_____

_____

2. Today I learned...

_____

3. Something amazing that happened today:

_____

Day: _____   Date: __/__/____

1. Today I am *Grateful* for:

_____

_____

_____

_____

2. Today I learned...

_____

3. Something amazing that happened today:

_____

Day: _____   Date: __/__/____

1. Today I am *Grateful* for:

_____

_____

_____

_____

2. Today I learned...

_____

3. Something amazing that happened today:

_____

Our life is what our thoughts make it.
— Marcus Aurelius

Day: _____   Date: __/__/____

1. Today I am *Grateful* for:

_____

_____

_____

_____

2. Today I learned...

_____

3. Something amazing that happened today:

_____

Day: _____   Date: __/__/____

1. Today I am *Grateful* for:

_____

_____

_____

_____

2. Today I learned...

_____

3. Something amazing that happened today:

_____

Day: _____   Date: __/__/____

1. Today I am *Grateful* for:

_____

_____

_____

_____

2. Today I learned...

_____

3. Something amazing that happened today:

_____

That man is a success who has lived well, laughed often
and loved much. — Robert Louis Stevenson

Day: _____   Date: _/_/___

1. Today I am *Grateful* for:

_____

_____

_____

_____

2. Today I learned...

_____

3. Something amazing that happened today:

_____

Day: _____   Date: _/_/___

1. Today I am *Grateful* for:

_____

_____

_____

_____

2. Today I learned...

_____

3. Something amazing that happened today:

_____

Day: _____   Date: _/_/___

1. Today I am *Grateful* for:

_____

_____

_____

_____

2. Today I learned...

_____

3. Something amazing that happened today:

_____

Life must be lived as play.
— Plato

Day: _____   Date: __/__/____

1. Today I am *Grateful* for:

_____

_____

_____

_____

2. Today I learned...

_____

3. Something amazing that happened today:

_____

Day: _____   Date: __/__/____

1. Today I am *Grateful* for:

_____

_____

_____

_____

2. Today I learned...

_____

3. Something amazing that happened today:

_____

Day: _____   Date: __/__/____

1. Today I am *Grateful* for:

_____

_____

_____

_____

2. Today I learned...

_____

3. Something amazing that happened today:

_____

Reasoning draws a conclusion, but does not make the conclusion certain, unless the mind discovers it by the path of experience.
— Roger Bacon

Day: _____   Date: __/__/___

1. Today I am *Grateful* for:

_____

_____

_____

_____

2. Today I learned...

_____

3. Something amazing that happened today:

_____

Day: _____   Date: __/__/___

1. Today I am *Grateful* for:

_____

_____

_____

_____

2. Today I learned...

_____

3. Something amazing that happened today:

_____

Day: _____   Date: __/__/___

1. Today I am *Grateful* for:

_____

_____

_____

_____

2. Today I learned...

_____

3. Something amazing that happened today:

_____

We consume our tomorrows fretting about our yesterdays.
— Persius

Day: _____   Date: __/__/____

1. Today I am *Grateful* for:

_____

_____

_____

_____

2. Today I learned...

_____

3. Something amazing that happened today:

_____

Day: _____   Date: __/__/____

1. Today I am *Grateful* for:

_____

_____

_____

_____

2. Today I learned...

_____

3. Something amazing that happened today:

_____

Day: _____   Date: __/__/____

1. Today I am *Grateful* for:

_____

_____

_____

_____

2. Today I learned...

_____

3. Something amazing that happened today:

_____

If the only prayer you ever say in your entire life is thank you,
it will be enough. — Meister Eckhart

Day: _____   Date: __/__/____

1. Today I am *Grateful* for:

_____

_____

_____

_____

2. Today I learned...

_____

3. Something amazing that happened today:

_____

Day: _____   Date: __/__/____

1. Today I am *Grateful* for:

_____

_____

_____

_____

2. Today I learned...

_____

3. Something amazing that happened today:

_____

Day: _____   Date: __/__/____

1. Today I am *Grateful* for:

_____

_____

_____

_____

2. Today I learned...

_____

3. Something amazing that happened today:

_____

Draw something

There is only one way to happiness and that is to cease worrying about things which are beyond the power of our will.
— Epictetus

Day: _____   Date: __/__/___

1. Today I am *Grateful* for:

_____
_____
_____
_____

2. Today I learned...

_____

3. Something amazing that happened today:

_____

Day: _____   Date: __/__/___

1. Today I am *Grateful* for:

_____
_____
_____
_____

2. Today I learned...

_____

3. Something amazing that happened today:

_____

Day: _____   Date: __/__/___

1. Today I am *Grateful* for:

_____
_____
_____
_____

2. Today I learned...

_____

3. Something amazing that happened today:

_____

It is during our darkest moments that we must focus
to see the light. — Aristotle

Day: _____   Date: __/__/___

1. Today I am *Grateful* for:

_____

_____

_____

_____

2. Today I learned...

_____

3. Something amazing that happened today:

_____

Day: _____   Date: __/__/___

1. Today I am *Grateful* for:

_____

_____

_____

_____

2. Today I learned...

_____

3. Something amazing that happened today:

_____

Day: _____   Date: __/__/___

1. Today I am *Grateful* for:

_____

_____

_____

_____

2. Today I learned...

_____

3. Something amazing that happened today:

_____

Things alter for the worse spontaneously, if they be not altered for the better designedly. — Francis Bacon

Day: _____   Date: __/__/___

1. Today I am *Grateful* for:

_____

_____

_____

_____

2. Today I learned...

_____

3. Something amazing that happened today:

_____

Day: _____   Date: __/__/___

1. Today I am *Grateful* for:

_____

_____

_____

_____

2. Today I learned...

_____

3. Something amazing that happened today:

_____

Day: _____   Date: __/__/___

1. Today I am *Grateful* for:

_____

_____

_____

_____

2. Today I learned...

_____

3. Something amazing that happened today:

_____

For the will and not the gift makes the giver.
— Gotthold Ephraim Lessing

Day: _____   Date: __/__/___

1. Today I am *Grateful* for:

_____

_____

_____

_____

2. Today I learned...

_____

3. Something amazing that happened today:

_____

Day: _____   Date: __/__/___

1. Today I am *Grateful* for:

_____

_____

_____

_____

2. Today I learned...

_____

3. Something amazing that happened today:

_____

Day: _____   Date: __/__/___

1. Today I am *Grateful* for:

_____

_____

_____

_____

2. Today I learned...

_____

3. Something amazing that happened today:

_____

We love life, not because we are used to living but because we are used to loving. — Friedrich Nietzsche

Day: _____   Date: __/__/____

1. Today I am *Grateful* for:

_____

_____

_____

_____

2. Today I learned...

_____

3. Something amazing that happened today:

_____

Day: _____   Date: __/__/____

1. Today I am *Grateful* for:

_____

_____

_____

_____

2. Today I learned...

_____

3. Something amazing that happened today:

_____

Day: _____   Date: __/__/____

1. Today I am *Grateful* for:

_____

_____

_____

_____

2. Today I learned...

_____

3. Something amazing that happened today:

_____

Ask me not what I have, but what I am.
— Heinrich Heine

Day: _____   Date: __/__/____

1. Today I am *Grateful* for:

_____
_____
_____
_____

2. Today I learned...

_____

3. Something amazing that happened today:

_____

Day: _____   Date: __/__/____

1. Today I am *Grateful* for:

_____
_____
_____
_____

2. Today I learned...

_____

3. Something amazing that happened today:

_____

Day: _____   Date: __/__/____

1. Today I am *Grateful* for:

_____
_____
_____
_____

2. Today I learned...

_____

3. Something amazing that happened today:

_____

A thing of beauty is a joy forever: its loveliness increases; it will never pass into nothingness. — John Keats

Day: _____   Date: __/__/___

1. Today I am *Grateful* for:

_____

_____

_____

_____

2. Today I learned...

_____

3. Something amazing that happened today:

_____

Day: _____   Date: __/__/___

1. Today I am *Grateful* for:

_____

_____

_____

_____

2. Today I learned...

_____

3. Something amazing that happened today:

_____

Day: _____   Date: __/__/___

1. Today I am *Grateful* for:

_____

_____

_____

_____

2. Today I learned...

_____

3. Something amazing that happened today:

_____

The power of imagination makes us infinite.
— John Muir

Day: _____   Date: __/__/___

1. Today I am *Grateful* for:

_____

_____

_____

_____

2. Today I learned...

_____

3. Something amazing that happened today:

_____

Day: _____   Date: __/__/___

1. Today I am *Grateful* for:

_____

_____

_____

_____

2. Today I learned...

_____

3. Something amazing that happened today:

_____

Day: _____   Date: __/__/___

1. Today I am *Grateful* for:

_____

_____

_____

_____

2. Today I learned...

_____

3. Something amazing that happened today:

_____

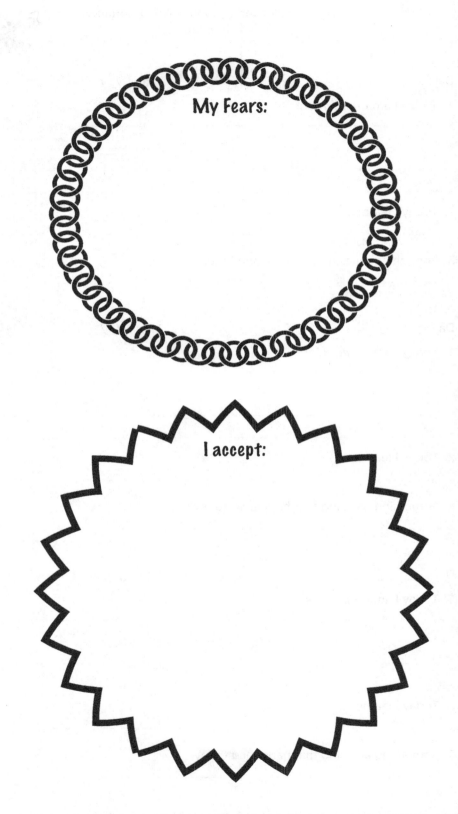

My Fears:

I accept:

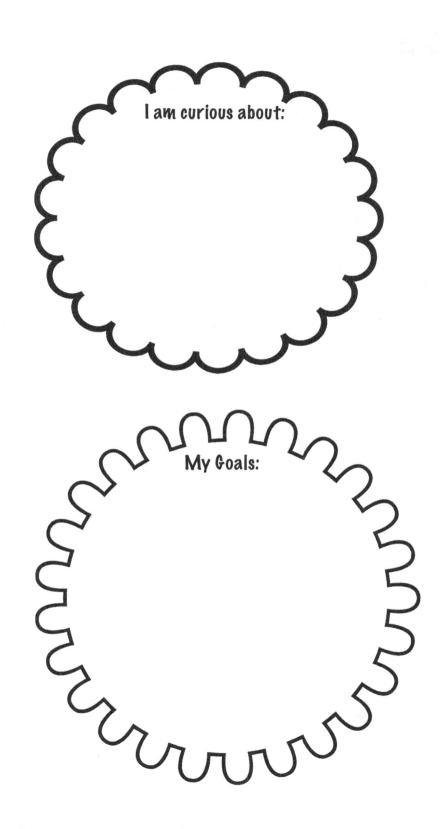

I am curious about:

My Goals:

Our greatest weakness lies in giving up. The most certain way to succeed is always to try just one more time.
— Thomas A. Edison

Day: _____   Date: __/__/___

1. Today I am *Grateful* for:

_____

_____

_____

_____

2. Today I learned...

_____

3. Something amazing that happened today:

_____

Day: _____   Date: __/__/___

1. Today I am *Grateful* for:

_____

_____

_____

_____

2. Today I learned...

_____

3. Something amazing that happened today:

_____

Day: _____   Date: __/__/___

1. Today I am *Grateful* for:

_____

_____

_____

_____

2. Today I learned...

_____

3. Something amazing that happened today:

_____

Draw something

The key is to keep company only with people who uplift you,
whose presence calls forth your best. — Epictetus

Day: _____   Date: __/__/___

1. Today I am *Grateful* for:

_____

_____

_____

_____

2. Today I learned...

_____

3. Something amazing that happened today:

_____

Day: _____   Date: __/__/___

1. Today I am *Grateful* for:

_____

_____

_____

_____

2. Today I learned...

_____

3. Something amazing that happened today:

_____

Day: _____   Date: __/__/___

1. Today I am *Grateful* for:

_____

_____

_____

_____

2. Today I learned...

_____

3. Something amazing that happened today:

_____

The one self-knowledge worth having is to know
one's own mind. — F. H. Bradley

Day: _____   Date: __/__/___

1. Today I am *Grateful* for:
_____
_____
_____
_____

2. Today I learned...
_____

3. Something amazing that happened today:
_____

Day: _____   Date: __/__/___

1. Today I am *Grateful* for:
_____
_____
_____
_____

2. Today I learned...
_____

3. Something amazing that happened today:
_____

Day: _____   Date: __/__/___

1. Today I am *Grateful* for:
_____
_____
_____
_____

2. Today I learned...
_____

3. Something amazing that happened today:
_____

If a little dreaming is dangerous, the cure for it is not to dream less but to dream more, to dream all the time. — Marcel Proust

Day: _____   Date: __/__/___

1. Today I am *Grateful* for:

_____

_____

_____

_____

2. Today I learned...

_____

3. Something amazing that happened today:

_____

Day: _____   Date: __/__/___

1. Today I am *Grateful* for:

_____

_____

_____

_____

2. Today I learned...

_____

3. Something amazing that happened today:

_____

Day: _____   Date: __/__/___

1. Today I am *Grateful* for:

_____

_____

_____

_____

2. Today I learned...

_____

3. Something amazing that happened today:

_____

He who knows others is wise. He who knows himself
is enlightened. — Lao Tzu

Day: _____   Date: _/_/___

1. Today I am *Grateful* for:

_____

_____

_____

_____

2. Today I learned...

_____

3. Something amazing that happened today:

_____

Day: _____   Date: _/_/___

1. Today I am *Grateful* for:

_____

_____

_____

_____

2. Today I learned...

_____

3. Something amazing that happened today:

_____

Day: _____   Date: _/_/___

1. Today I am *Grateful* for:

_____

_____

_____

_____

2. Today I learned...

_____

3. Something amazing that happened today:

_____

There are two ways of spreading light: to be the candle or the mirror that reflects it. — Edith Wharton

Day: _____   Date: __/__/___

1. Today I am *Grateful* for:

_____

_____

_____

_____

2. Today I learned...

_____

3. Something amazing that happened today:

_____

Day: _____   Date: __/__/___

1. Today I am *Grateful* for:

_____

_____

_____

_____

2. Today I learned...

_____

3. Something amazing that happened today:

_____

Day: _____   Date: __/__/___

1. Today I am *Grateful* for:

_____

_____

_____

_____

2. Today I learned...

_____

3. Something amazing that happened today:

_____

The strongest principle of growth lies in the human choice.
— George Eliot

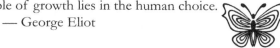

Day: _____   Date: __/__/___

1. Today I am *Grateful* for:

_____

_____

_____

_____

2. Today I learned...

_____

3. Something amazing that happened today:

_____

Day: _____   Date: __/__/___

1. Today I am *Grateful* for:

_____

_____

_____

_____

2. Today I learned...

_____

3. Something amazing that happened today:

_____

Day: _____   Date: __/__/___

1. Today I am *Grateful* for:

_____

_____

_____

_____

2. Today I learned...

_____

3. Something amazing that happened today:

_____

Success usually comes to those who are too busy
to be looking for it. — Henry David Thoreau

Day: _____   Date: __/__/___

1. Today I am *Grateful* for:

_____

_____

_____

2. Today I learned...

_____

3. Something amazing that happened today:

_____

Day: _____   Date: __/__/___

1. Today I am *Grateful* for:

_____

_____

_____

2. Today I learned...

_____

3. Something amazing that happened today:

_____

Day: _____   Date: __/__/___

1. Today I am *Grateful* for:

_____

_____

_____

2. Today I learned...

_____

3. Something amazing that happened today:

_____

If we learn not humility, we learn nothing.
— John Jewel

Day: _____   Date: __/__/___

1. Today I am *Grateful* for:

_____

_____

_____

_____

2. Today I learned...

_____

3. Something amazing that happened today:

_____

Day: _____   Date: __/__/___

1. Today I am *Grateful* for:

_____

_____

_____

_____

2. Today I learned...

_____

3. Something amazing that happened today:

_____

Day: _____   Date: __/__/___

1. Today I am *Grateful* for:

_____

_____

_____

_____

2. Today I learned...

_____

3. Something amazing that happened today:

_____

Keep your face always toward the sunshine - and
shadows will fall behind you. — Walt Whitman

Day: _____   Date: __/__/____

1. Today I am *Grateful* for:

_____

_____

_____

_____

2. Today I learned...

_____

3. Something amazing that happened today:

_____

Day: _____   Date: __/__/____

1. Today I am *Grateful* for:

_____

_____

_____

_____

2. Today I learned...

_____

3. Something amazing that happened today:

_____

Day: _____   Date: __/__/____

1. Today I am *Grateful* for:

_____

_____

_____

_____

2. Today I learned...

_____

3. Something amazing that happened today:

_____

Draw something

Beauty surrounds us, but usually we need to be
walking in a garden to know it. — Rumi

Day: _____   Date: _/_/___

1. Today I am *Grateful* for:

_____

_____

_____

_____

2. Today I learned...

_____

3. Something amazing that happened today:

_____

Day: _____   Date: _/_/___

1. Today I am *Grateful* for:

_____

_____

_____

_____

2. Today I learned...

_____

3. Something amazing that happened today:

_____

Day: _____   Date: _/_/___

1. Today I am *Grateful* for:

_____

_____

_____

_____

2. Today I learned...

_____

3. Something amazing that happened today:

_____

The thankful receiver bears a plentiful harvest.
— William Blake

Day: _____   Date: __/__/___

1. Today I am *Grateful* for:

_____

_____

_____

_____

2. Today I learned...

_____

3. Something amazing that happened today:

_____

Day: _____   Date: __/__/___

1. Today I am *Grateful* for:

_____

_____

_____

_____

2. Today I learned...

_____

3. Something amazing that happened today:

_____

Day: _____   Date: __/__/___

1. Today I am *Grateful* for:

_____

_____

_____

_____

2. Today I learned...

_____

3. Something amazing that happened today:

_____

To know, is to know that you know nothing. That is the meaning of true knowledge. — Socrates

Day: _____   Date: __/__/___

1. Today I am *Grateful* for:

_____

_____

_____

_____

2. Today I learned...

_____

3. Something amazing that happened today:

_____

Day: _____   Date: __/__/___

1. Today I am *Grateful* for:

_____

_____

_____

_____

2. Today I learned...

_____

3. Something amazing that happened today:

_____

Day: _____   Date: __/__/___

1. Today I am *Grateful* for:

_____

_____

_____

_____

2. Today I learned...

_____

3. Something amazing that happened today:

_____

Either I will find a way, or I will make one.
— Philip Sidney

Day: _____   Date: __/__/____

1. Today I am *Grateful* for:
_____
_____
_____
_____

2. Today I learned...
_____

3. Something amazing that happened today:
_____

Day: _____   Date: __/__/____

1. Today I am *Grateful* for:
_____
_____
_____
_____

2. Today I learned...
_____

3. Something amazing that happened today:
_____

Day: _____   Date: __/__/____

1. Today I am *Grateful* for:
_____
_____
_____
_____

2. Today I learned...
_____

3. Something amazing that happened today:
_____

Write it on your heart that every day is the best day in the year.
— Ralph Waldo Emerson

Day: _____   Date: _/_/___

1. Today I am *Grateful* for:

_____

_____

_____

_____

2. Today I learned...

_____

3. Something amazing that happened today:

_____

Day: _____   Date: _/_/___

1. Today I am *Grateful* for:

_____

_____

_____

_____

2. Today I learned...

_____

3. Something amazing that happened today:

_____

Day: _____   Date: _/_/___

1. Today I am *Grateful* for:

_____

_____

_____

_____

2. Today I learned...

_____

3. Something amazing that happened today:

_____

Lend yourself to others, but give yourself to yourself.
— Michel de Montaigne

Day: _____

Date: _/_/___

1. Today I am *Grateful* for:

_____

_____

_____

_____

2. Today I learned...

_____

3. Something amazing that happened today:

_____

Day: _____

Date: _/_/___

1. Today I am *Grateful* for:

_____

_____

_____

_____

2. Today I learned...

_____

3. Something amazing that happened today:

_____

Day: _____

Date: _/_/___

1. Today I am *Grateful* for:

_____

_____

_____

_____

2. Today I learned...

_____

3. Something amazing that happened today:

_____

Little minds are interested in the extraordinary; great minds
in the commonplace. — Elbert Hubbard

Day: _____   Date: __/__/____

1. Today I am *Grateful* for:

_____

_____

_____

_____

2. Today I learned...

_____

3. Something amazing that happened today:

_____

Day: _____   Date: __/__/____

1. Today I am *Grateful* for:

_____

_____

_____

_____

2. Today I learned...

_____

3. Something amazing that happened today:

_____

Day: _____   Date: __/__/____

1. Today I am *Grateful* for:

_____

_____

_____

_____

2. Today I learned...

_____

3. Something amazing that happened today:

_____

If there is no struggle, there is no progress.
— Frederick Douglass

Day: _____   Date: _/_/___

1. Today I am *Grateful* for:
_____

_____

_____

_____

2. Today I learned...
_____

3. Something amazing that happened today:
_____

Day: _____   Date: _/_/___

1. Today I am *Grateful* for:
_____

_____

_____

_____

2. Today I learned...
_____

3. Something amazing that happened today:
_____

Day: _____   Date: _/_/___

1. Today I am *Grateful* for:
_____

_____

_____

_____

2. Today I learned...
_____

3. Something amazing that happened today:
_____

The dawn is not distant, nor is the night starless; love is eternal.
— Henry Wadsworth Longfellow

Day: _____   Date: __/__/___

1. Today I am *Grateful* for:

_____
_____
_____
_____

2. Today I learned...

_____

3. Something amazing that happened today:

_____

Day: _____   Date: __/__/___

1. Today I am *Grateful* for:

_____
_____
_____
_____

2. Today I learned...

_____

3. Something amazing that happened today:

_____

Day: _____   Date: __/__/___

1. Today I am *Grateful* for:

_____
_____
_____
_____

2. Today I learned...

_____

3. Something amazing that happened today:

_____

Draw something

Never give up, for that is just the place and time
that the tide will turn. — Harriet Beecher Stowe

Day: _____   Date: __/__/____

1. Today I am *Grateful* for:

_____

_____

_____

_____

2. Today I learned...

_____

3. Something amazing that happened today:

_____

Day: _____   Date: __/__/____

1. Today I am *Grateful* for:

_____

_____

_____

_____

2. Today I learned...

_____

3. Something amazing that happened today:

_____

Day: _____   Date: __/__/____

1. Today I am *Grateful* for:

_____

_____

_____

_____

2. Today I learned...

_____

3. Something amazing that happened today:

_____

Day: _____   Date: __/__/____

1. Today I am *Grateful* for:

_____

_____

_____

_____

2. Today I learned...

_____

3. Something amazing that happened today:

_____

Day: _____   Date: __/__/____

1. Today I am *Grateful* for:

_____

_____

_____

_____

2. Today I learned...

_____

3. Something amazing that happened today:

_____

Day: _____   Date: __/__/____

1. Today I am *Grateful* for:

_____

_____

_____

_____

2. Today I learned...

_____

3. Something amazing that happened today:

_____

No act of kindness, no matter how small, is ever wasted.
— Aesop

Day: _____   Date: __/__/___

1. Today I am *Grateful* for:

_____

_____

_____

_____

2. Today I learned...

_____

3. Something amazing that happened today:

_____

Day: _____   Date: __/__/___

1. Today I am *Grateful* for:

_____

_____

_____

_____

2. Today I learned...

_____

3. Something amazing that happened today:

_____

Day: _____   Date: __/__/___

1. Today I am *Grateful* for:

_____

_____

_____

_____

2. Today I learned...

_____

3. Something amazing that happened today:

_____

Doubt comes in at the window when inquiry is denied at the door. — Benjamin Jowett

Day: _____   Date: __/__/___

1. Today I am *Grateful* for:
_____
_____
_____
_____

2. Today I learned...
_____

3. Something amazing that happened today:
_____

Day: _____   Date: __/__/___

1. Today I am *Grateful* for:
_____
_____
_____
_____

2. Today I learned...
_____

3. Something amazing that happened today:
_____

Day: _____   Date: __/__/___

1. Today I am *Grateful* for:
_____
_____
_____
_____

2. Today I learned...
_____

3. Something amazing that happened today:
_____

Make it your habit not to be critical about small things.
— Edward Everett Hale

Day: _____   Date: _/_/_

1. Today I am *Grateful* for:

_____

_____

_____

_____

2. Today I learned...

_____

3. Something amazing that happened today:

_____

Day: _____   Date: _/_/_

1. Today I am *Grateful* for:

_____

_____

_____

_____

2. Today I learned...

_____

3. Something amazing that happened today:

_____

Day: _____   Date: _/_/_

1. Today I am *Grateful* for:

_____

_____

_____

_____

2. Today I learned...

_____

3. Something amazing that happened today:

_____

Genius is patience.
— Isaac Newton

Day: _____   Date: __/__/___

1. Today I am *Grateful* for:

_____

_____

_____

_____

2. Today I learned...

_____

3. Something amazing that happened today:

_____

Day: _____   Date: __/__/___

1. Today I am *Grateful* for:

_____

_____

_____

_____

2. Today I learned...

_____

3. Something amazing that happened today:

_____

Day: _____   Date: __/__/___

1. Today I am *Grateful* for:

_____

_____

_____

_____

2. Today I learned...

_____

3. Something amazing that happened today:

_____

A thousand words will not leave so deep an
impression as one deed. — Henrik Ibsen

Day: _____   Date: __/__/___

1. Today I am *Grateful* for:
_____
_____
_____
_____

2. Today I learned...
_____

3. Something amazing that happened today:
_____

Day: _____   Date: __/__/___

1. Today I am *Grateful* for:
_____
_____
_____
_____

2. Today I learned...
_____

3. Something amazing that happened today:
_____

Day: _____   Date: __/__/___

1. Today I am *Grateful* for:
_____
_____
_____
_____

2. Today I learned...
_____

3. Something amazing that happened today:
_____

Remember when life's path is steep to keep your mind even.
— Horace

Day: _____   Date: __/__/___

1. Today I am *Grateful* for:

_____

_____

_____

_____

2. Today I learned...

_____

3. Something amazing that happened today:

_____

Day: _____   Date: __/__/___

1. Today I am *Grateful* for:

_____

_____

_____

_____

2. Today I learned...

_____

3. Something amazing that happened today:

_____

Day: _____   Date: __/__/___

1. Today I am *Grateful* for:

_____

_____

_____

_____

2. Today I learned...

_____

3. Something amazing that happened today:

_____

If you wish to reach the highest, begin at the lowest.
— Publilius Syrus

Day: _____   Date: __/__/____

1. Today I am *Grateful* for:

_____

_____

_____

_____

2. Today I learned...

_____

3. Something amazing that happened today:

_____

Day: _____   Date: __/__/____

1. Today I am *Grateful* for:

_____

_____

_____

_____

2. Today I learned...

_____

3. Something amazing that happened today:

_____

Day: _____   Date: __/__/____

1. Today I am *Grateful* for:

_____

_____

_____

_____

2. Today I learned...

_____

3. Something amazing that happened today:

_____

Draw something

By appreciation, we make excellence in others our own property.
— Voltaire

Day: _____ Date: _/_/___

1. Today I am *Grateful* for:

_____

_____

_____

_____

2. Today I learned...

_____

3. Something amazing that happened today:

_____

Day: _____ Date: _/_/___

1. Today I am *Grateful* for:

_____

_____

_____

_____

2. Today I learned...

_____

3. Something amazing that happened today:

_____

Day: _____ Date: _/_/___

1. Today I am *Grateful* for:

_____

_____

_____

_____

2. Today I learned...

_____

3. Something amazing that happened today:

_____

Act as if what you do makes a difference. It does.
— William James

Day: _____   Date: __/__/___

1. Today I am *Grateful* for:

_____

_____

_____

_____

2. Today I learned...

_____

3. Something amazing that happened today:

_____

Day: _____   Date: __/__/___

1. Today I am *Grateful* for:

_____

_____

_____

_____

2. Today I learned...

_____

3. Something amazing that happened today:

_____

Day: _____   Date: __/__/___

1. Today I am *Grateful* for:

_____

_____

_____

_____

2. Today I learned...

_____

3. Something amazing that happened today:

_____

We are here to add what we can to life, not to get what
we can from life. — William Osler

Day: _____   Date: __/__/___

1. Today I am *Grateful* for:

_____

_____

_____

_____

2. Today I learned...

_____

3. Something amazing that happened today:

_____

Day: _____   Date: __/__/___

1. Today I am *Grateful* for:

_____

_____

_____

_____

2. Today I learned...

_____

3. Something amazing that happened today:

_____

Day: _____   Date: __/__/___

1. Today I am *Grateful* for:

_____

_____

_____

_____

2. Today I learned...

_____

3. Something amazing that happened today:

_____

Success is dependent on effort.
— Sophocles

Day: _____   Date: __/__/____

1. Today I am *Grateful* for:

_____
_____
_____
_____

2. Today I learned...

_____

3. Something amazing that happened today:

_____

Day: _____   Date: __/__/____

1. Today I am *Grateful* for:

_____
_____
_____
_____

2. Today I learned...

_____

3. Something amazing that happened today:

_____

Day: _____   Date: __/__/____

1. Today I am *Grateful* for:

_____
_____
_____
_____

2. Today I learned...

_____

3. Something amazing that happened today:

_____

*I hear and I forget. I see and I remember. I do
and I understand.* — Confucius

Day: _____   Date: __/__/____

1. Today I am *Grateful* for:

_____

_____

_____

_____

2. Today I learned...

_____

3. Something amazing that happened today:

_____

Day: _____   Date: __/__/____

1. Today I am *Grateful* for:

_____

_____

_____

_____

2. Today I learned...

_____

3. Something amazing that happened today:

_____

Day: _____   Date: __/__/____

1. Today I am *Grateful* for:

_____

_____

_____

_____

2. Today I learned...

_____

3. Something amazing that happened today:

_____

Reality is what you can count on.
— Dallas Willard

Day: _____   Date: __/__/___

1. Today I am *Grateful* for:

_____

_____

_____

_____

2. Today I learned...

_____

3. Something amazing that happened today:

_____

Day: _____   Date: __/__/___

1. Today I am *Grateful* for:

_____

_____

_____

_____

2. Today I learned...

_____

3. Something amazing that happened today:

_____

Day: _____   Date: __/__/___

1. Today I am *Grateful* for:

_____

_____

_____

_____

2. Today I learned...

_____

3. Something amazing that happened today:

_____

Creativity is not the finding of a thing, but the making something
out of it after it is found. — James Russell Lowell

Day: _____   Date: __/__/___

1. Today I am *Grateful* for:

_____

_____

_____

_____

2. Today I learned...

_____

3. Something amazing that happened today:

_____

Day: _____   Date: __/__/___

1. Today I am *Grateful* for:

_____

_____

_____

_____

2. Today I learned...

_____

3. Something amazing that happened today:

_____

Day: _____   Date: __/__/___

1. Today I am *Grateful* for:

_____

_____

_____

_____

2. Today I learned...

_____

3. Something amazing that happened today:

_____

In every walk with nature one receives far more
than he seeks. — John Muir

Day: _____   Date: __/__/___

1. Today I am *Grateful* for:

_____

_____

_____

_____

2. Today I learned...

_____

3. Something amazing that happened today:

_____

Day: _____   Date: __/__/___

1. Today I am *Grateful* for:

_____

_____

_____

_____

2. Today I learned...

_____

3. Something amazing that happened today:

_____

Day: _____   Date: __/__/___

1. Today I am *Grateful* for:

_____

_____

_____

_____

2. Today I learned...

_____

3. Something amazing that happened today:

_____

Success consists of getting up just one more time than you fall.
— Oliver Goldsmith

Day: _____   Date: _/_/___

1. Today I am *Grateful* for:
_____
_____
_____
_____

2. Today I learned...
_____

3. Something amazing that happened today:
_____

Day: _____   Date: _/_/___

1. Today I am *Grateful* for:
_____
_____
_____
_____

2. Today I learned...
_____

3. Something amazing that happened today:
_____

Day: _____   Date: _/_/___

1. Today I am *Grateful* for:
_____
_____
_____
_____

2. Today I learned...
_____

3. Something amazing that happened today:
_____

Draw something

We do not see nature with our eyes, but with our understandings and our hearts. — William Hazlitt

Day: _____   Date: __/__/____

1. Today I am *Grateful* for:

_____

_____

_____

_____

2. Today I learned...

_____

3. Something amazing that happened today:

_____

Day: _____   Date: __/__/____

1. Today I am *Grateful* for:

_____

_____

_____

_____

2. Today I learned...

_____

3. Something amazing that happened today:

_____

Day: _____   Date: __/__/____

1. Today I am *Grateful* for:

_____

_____

_____

_____

2. Today I learned...

_____

3. Something amazing that happened today:

_____

Excessive fear is always powerless.
— Aeschylus

Day: _____   Date: __/__/___

1. Today I am *Grateful* for:

_____

_____

_____

_____

2. Today I learned...

_____

3. Something amazing that happened today:

_____

Day: _____   Date: __/__/___

1. Today I am *Grateful* for:

_____

_____

_____

_____

2. Today I learned...

_____

3. Something amazing that happened today:

_____

Day: _____   Date: __/__/___

1. Today I am *Grateful* for:

_____

_____

_____

_____

2. Today I learned...

_____

3. Something amazing that happened today:

_____

Grace is the beauty of form under the influence of freedom.
— Friedrich Schiller

Day: _____   Date: _/_/___

1. Today I am *Grateful* for:

_____

_____

_____

_____

2. Today I learned...

_____

3. Something amazing that happened today:

_____

Day: _____   Date: _/_/___

1. Today I am *Grateful* for:

_____

_____

_____

_____

2. Today I learned...

_____

3. Something amazing that happened today:

_____

Day: _____   Date: _/_/___

1. Today I am *Grateful* for:

_____

_____

_____

_____

2. Today I learned...

_____

3. Something amazing that happened today:

_____

Brevity is a great charm of eloquence.
— Marcus Tullius Cicero

Day: _____   Date: __/__/___

1. Today I am *Grateful* for:
_____
_____
_____
_____

2. Today I learned...
_____

3. Something amazing that happened today:
_____

Day: _____   Date: __/__/___

1. Today I am *Grateful* for:
_____
_____
_____
_____

2. Today I learned...
_____

3. Something amazing that happened today:
_____

Day: _____   Date: __/__/___

1. Today I am *Grateful* for:
_____
_____
_____
_____

2. Today I learned...
_____

3. Something amazing that happened today:
_____

Genius is the ability to renew one's emotions in daily experience.
— Paul Cezanne

Day: _____   Date: __/__/____

1. Today I am *Grateful* for:

_____

_____

_____

_____

2. Today I learned...

_____

3. Something amazing that happened today:

_____

Day: _____   Date: __/__/____

1. Today I am *Grateful* for:

_____

_____

_____

_____

2. Today I learned...

_____

3. Something amazing that happened today:

_____

Day: _____   Date: __/__/____

1. Today I am *Grateful* for:

_____

_____

_____

_____

2. Today I learned...

_____

3. Something amazing that happened today:

_____

Day: _____   Date: _/_/___

1. Today I am *Grateful* for:

_____

_____

_____

_____

2. Today I learned...

_____

3. Something amazing that happened today:

_____

Day: _____   Date: _/_/___

1. Today I am *Grateful* for:

_____

_____

_____

_____

2. Today I learned...

_____

3. Something amazing that happened today:

_____

Day: _____   Date: _/_/___

1. Today I am *Grateful* for:

_____

_____

_____

_____

2. Today I learned...

_____

3. Something amazing that happened today:

_____

Tears of joy are like the summer rain drops pierced by sunbeams.
— Hosea Ballou

Day: _____   Date: __/__/____

1. Today I am *Grateful* for:

_____

_____

_____

_____

2. Today I learned...

_____

3. Something amazing that happened today:

_____

Day: _____   Date: __/__/____

1. Today I am *Grateful* for:

_____

_____

_____

_____

2. Today I learned...

_____

3. Something amazing that happened today:

_____

Day: _____   Date: __/__/____

1. Today I am *Grateful* for:

_____

_____

_____

_____

2. Today I learned...

_____

3. Something amazing that happened today:

_____

What we achieve inwardly will change outer reality.
— Plutarch

Day: _____   Date: __/__/___

1. Today I am *Grateful* for:

_____

_____

_____

_____

2. Today I learned...

_____

3. Something amazing that happened today:

_____

Day: _____   Date: __/__/___

1. Today I am *Grateful* for:

_____

_____

_____

_____

2. Today I learned...

_____

3. Something amazing that happened today:

_____

Day: _____   Date: __/__/___

1. Today I am *Grateful* for:

_____

_____

_____

_____

2. Today I learned...

_____

3. Something amazing that happened today:

_____

It is costly wisdom that is bought by experience.
— Roger Ascham

Day: _____   Date: _/_/___

1. Today I am *Grateful* for:

_____

_____

_____

_____

2. Today I learned...

_____

3. Something amazing that happened today:

_____

Day: _____   Date: _/_/___

1. Today I am *Grateful* for:

_____

_____

_____

_____

2. Today I learned...

_____

3. Something amazing that happened today:

_____

Day: _____   Date: _/_/___

1. Today I am *Grateful* for:

_____

_____

_____

_____

2. Today I learned...

_____

3. Something amazing that happened today:

_____

Draw something

There is nothing like a dream to create the future.
— Victor Hugo

Day: _____   Date: _/_/___

1. Today I am *Grateful* for:

_____

_____

_____

_____

2. Today I learned...

_____

3. Something amazing that happened today:

_____

Day: _____   Date: _/_/___

1. Today I am *Grateful* for:

_____

_____

_____

_____

2. Today I learned...

_____

3. Something amazing that happened today:

_____

Day: _____   Date: _/_/___

1. Today I am *Grateful* for:

_____

_____

_____

_____

2. Today I learned...

_____

3. Something amazing that happened today:

_____

The future is purchased by the present.
— Samuel Johnson

Day: _____   Date: __/__/____

1. Today I am *Grateful* for:

_____

_____

_____

_____

2. Today I learned...

_____

3. Something amazing that happened today:

_____

Day: _____   Date: __/__/____

1. Today I am *Grateful* for:

_____

_____

_____

_____

2. Today I learned...

_____

3. Something amazing that happened today:

_____

Day: _____   Date: __/__/____

1. Today I am *Grateful* for:

_____

_____

_____

_____

2. Today I learned...

_____

3. Something amazing that happened today:

_____

Life can only be understood backwards; but it must
be lived forwards. — Soren Kierkegaard

Day: _____   Date: __/__/____

1. Today I am *Grateful* for:

_____

_____

_____

_____

2. Today I learned...

_____

3. Something amazing that happened today:

_____

Day: _____   Date: __/__/____

1. Today I am *Grateful* for:

_____

_____

_____

_____

2. Today I learned...

_____

3. Something amazing that happened today:

_____

Day: _____   Date: __/__/____

1. Today I am *Grateful* for:

_____

_____

_____

_____

2. Today I learned...

_____

3. Something amazing that happened today:

_____

A friend is a gift you give yourself.
— Robert Louis Stevenson

Day: _____   Date: __/__/___

1. Today I am *Grateful* for:

_____

_____

_____

_____

2. Today I learned...

_____

3. Something amazing that happened today:

_____

Day: _____   Date: __/__/___

1. Today I am *Grateful* for:

_____

_____

_____

_____

2. Today I learned...

_____

3. Something amazing that happened today:

_____

Day: _____   Date: __/__/___

1. Today I am *Grateful* for:

_____

_____

_____

_____

2. Today I learned...

_____

3. Something amazing that happened today:

_____

No man is an island, entire of itself; every man is a
piece of the continent. — John Donne

Day: _____   Date: _/_/___

1. Today I am *Grateful* for:

_____

_____

_____

_____

2. Today I learned...

_____

3. Something amazing that happened today:

_____

Day: _____   Date: _/_/___

1. Today I am *Grateful* for:

_____

_____

_____

_____

2. Today I learned...

_____

3. Something amazing that happened today:

_____

Day: _____   Date: _/_/___

1. Today I am *Grateful* for:

_____

_____

_____

_____

2. Today I learned...

_____

3. Something amazing that happened today:

_____

To love oneself is the beginning of a lifelong romance.
— Oscar Wilde

Day: _____   Date: __/__/____

1. Today I am *Grateful* for:

_____

_____

_____

_____

2. Today I learned...

_____

3. Something amazing that happened today:

_____

Day: _____   Date: __/__/____

1. Today I am *Grateful* for:

_____

_____

_____

_____

2. Today I learned...

_____

3. Something amazing that happened today:

_____

Day: _____   Date: __/__/____

1. Today I am *Grateful* for:

_____

_____

_____

_____

2. Today I learned...

_____

3. Something amazing that happened today:

_____

As people are walking all the time, in the same spot,
a path appears. — John Locke

Day: _____   Date: __/__/____

1. Today I am *Grateful* for:

_____

_____

_____

_____

2. Today I learned...

_____

3. Something amazing that happened today:

_____

Day: _____   Date: __/__/____

1. Today I am *Grateful* for:

_____

_____

_____

_____

2. Today I learned...

_____

3. Something amazing that happened today:

_____

Day: _____   Date: __/__/____

1. Today I am *Grateful* for:

_____

_____

_____

_____

2. Today I learned...

_____

3. Something amazing that happened today:

_____

Nothing great was ever achieved without enthusiasm.
— Ralph Waldo Emerson

Day: _____   Date: _/_/___

1. Today I am *Grateful* for:

_____

_____

_____

_____

2. Today I learned...

_____

3. Something amazing that happened today:

_____

Day: _____   Date: _/_/___

1. Today I am *Grateful* for:

_____

_____

_____

_____

2. Today I learned...

_____

3. Something amazing that happened today:

_____

Day: _____   Date: _/_/___

1. Today I am *Grateful* for:

_____

_____

_____

_____

2. Today I learned...

_____

3. Something amazing that happened today:

_____

Who knows, the mind has the key to all things besides.
— Amos Bronson Alcott

Day: _____   Date: __/__/___

1. Today I am *Grateful* for:

_____

_____

_____

_____

2. Today I learned...

_____

3. Something amazing that happened today:

_____

Day: _____   Date: __/__/___

1. Today I am *Grateful* for:

_____

_____

_____

_____

2. Today I learned...

_____

3. Something amazing that happened today:

_____

Day: _____   Date: __/__/___

1. Today I am *Grateful* for:

_____

_____

_____

_____

2. Today I learned...

_____

3. Something amazing that happened today:

_____

Draw something

Of the blessings set before you make your choice,
and be content. — Samuel Johnson

Day: _____   Date: __/__/____

1. Today I am *Grateful* for:

_____

_____

_____

_____

2. Today I learned...

_____

3. Something amazing that happened today:

_____

Day: _____   Date: __/__/____

1. Today I am *Grateful* for:

_____

_____

_____

_____

2. Today I learned...

_____

3. Something amazing that happened today:

_____

Day: _____   Date: __/__/____

1. Today I am *Grateful* for:

_____

_____

_____

_____

2. Today I learned...

_____

3. Something amazing that happened today:

_____

Beauty is not caused. It is.
— Emily Dickinson

Day: _____   Date: __/__/____

1. Today I am *Grateful* for:

_____

_____

_____

_____

2. Today I learned...

_____

3. Something amazing that happened today:

_____

Day: _____   Date: __/__/____

1. Today I am *Grateful* for:

_____

_____

_____

_____

2. Today I learned...

_____

3. Something amazing that happened today:

_____

Day: _____   Date: __/__/____

1. Today I am *Grateful* for:

_____

_____

_____

_____

2. Today I learned...

_____

3. Something amazing that happened today:

_____

We feel and know that we are eternal.
— Baruch Spinoza

Day: _____   Date: __/__/___

1. Today I am *Grateful* for:

_____

_____

_____

_____

2. Today I learned...

_____

3. Something amazing that happened today:

_____

Day: _____   Date: __/__/___

1. Today I am *Grateful* for:

_____

_____

_____

_____

2. Today I learned...

_____

3. Something amazing that happened today:

_____

Day: _____   Date: __/__/___

1. Today I am *Grateful* for:

_____

_____

_____

_____

2. Today I learned...

_____

3. Something amazing that happened today:

_____

The things that we love tell us what we are.
— Thomas Aquinas

Day: _____   Date: __/__/____

1. Today I am *Grateful* for:
_____
_____
_____
_____

2. Today I learned...
_____

3. Something amazing that happened today:
_____

Day: _____   Date: __/__/____

1. Today I am *Grateful* for:
_____
_____
_____
_____

2. Today I learned...
_____

3. Something amazing that happened today:
_____

Day: _____   Date: __/__/____

1. Today I am *Grateful* for:
_____
_____
_____
_____

2. Today I learned...
_____

3. Something amazing that happened today:
_____

The way to know life is to love many things.
— Vincent Van Gogh

Day: _____   Date: __/__/____

1. Today I am *Grateful* for:

_____

_____

_____

_____

2. Today I learned...

_____

3. Something amazing that happened today:

_____

Day: _____   Date: __/__/____

1. Today I am *Grateful* for:

_____

_____

_____

_____

2. Today I learned...

_____

3. Something amazing that happened today:

_____

Day: _____   Date: __/__/____

1. Today I am *Grateful* for:

_____

_____

_____

_____

2. Today I learned...

_____

3. Something amazing that happened today:

_____

Our opportunities to do good are our talents.
— Cotton Mather

Day: _____   Date: __/__/___

1. Today I am *Grateful* for:

_____

_____

_____

_____

2. Today I learned...

_____

3. Something amazing that happened today:

_____

Day: _____   Date: __/__/___

1. Today I am *Grateful* for:

_____

_____

_____

_____

2. Today I learned...

_____

3. Something amazing that happened today:

_____

Day: _____   Date: __/__/___

1. Today I am *Grateful* for:

_____

_____

_____

_____

2. Today I learned...

_____

3. Something amazing that happened today:

_____

The eye sees what it brings the power to see.
— Thomas Carlyle

Day: _____   Date: __/__/___

1. Today I am *Grateful* for:

_____

_____

_____

_____

2. Today I learned...

_____

3. Something amazing that happened today:

_____

Day: _____   Date: __/__/___

1. Today I am *Grateful* for:

_____

_____

_____

_____

2. Today I learned...

_____

3. Something amazing that happened today:

_____

Day: _____   Date: __/__/___

1. Today I am *Grateful* for:

_____

_____

_____

_____

2. Today I learned...

_____

3. Something amazing that happened today:

_____

The purpose creates the machine.
— Arthur Young

Day: _____   Date: __/__/___

1. Today I am *Grateful* for:
_____
_____
_____
_____

2. Today I learned...
_____

3. Something amazing that happened today:
_____

Day: _____   Date: __/__/___

1. Today I am *Grateful* for:
_____
_____
_____
_____

2. Today I learned...
_____

3. Something amazing that happened today:
_____

Day: _____   Date: __/__/___

1. Today I am *Grateful* for:
_____
_____
_____
_____

2. Today I learned...
_____

3. Something amazing that happened today:
_____

They can conquer who believe they can.
— Virgil

Day: _____   Date: __/__/___

1. Today I am *Grateful* for:

_____

_____

_____

_____

2. Today I learned...

_____

3. Something amazing that happened today:

_____

Day: _____   Date: __/__/___

1. Today I am *Grateful* for:

_____

_____

_____

_____

2. Today I learned...

_____

3. Something amazing that happened today:

_____

Day: _____   Date: __/__/___

1. Today I am *Grateful* for:

_____

_____

_____

_____

2. Today I learned...

_____

3. Something amazing that happened today:

_____

Draw something

No man ever steps in the same river twice, for it's not the same river and he's not the same man. — Heraclitus

Day: _____   Date: __/__/___

1. Today I am *Grateful* for:

_____

_____

_____

_____

2. Today I learned...

_____

3. Something amazing that happened today:

_____

Day: _____   Date: __/__/___

1. Today I am *Grateful* for:

_____

_____

_____

_____

2. Today I learned...

_____

3. Something amazing that happened today:

_____

Day: _____   Date: __/__/___

1. Today I am *Grateful* for:

_____

_____

_____

_____

2. Today I learned...

_____

3. Something amazing that happened today:

_____

He has the most who is most content with the least.
— Diogenes

Day: _____   Date: _/_/___

1. Today I am *Grateful* for:

_____

_____

_____

_____

2. Today I learned...

_____

3. Something amazing that happened today:

_____

Day: _____   Date: _/_/___

1. Today I am *Grateful* for:

_____

_____

_____

_____

2. Today I learned...

_____

3. Something amazing that happened today:

_____

Day: _____   Date: _/_/___

1. Today I am *Grateful* for:

_____

_____

_____

_____

2. Today I learned...

_____

3. Something amazing that happened today:

_____

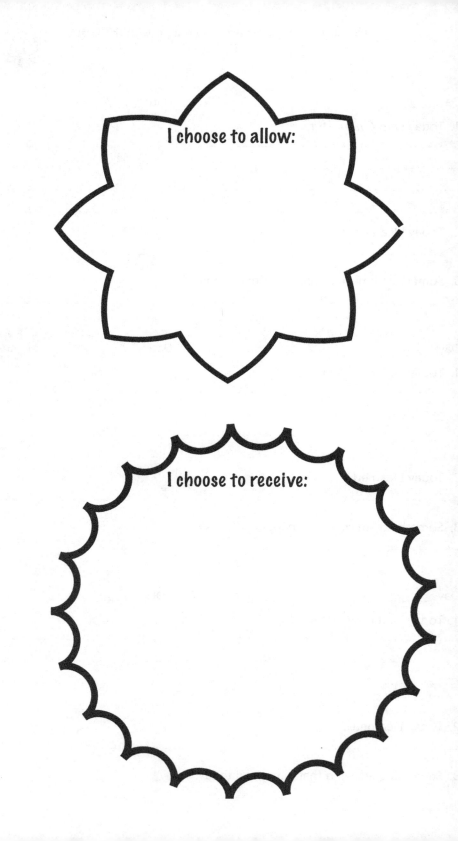

I choose to allow:

I choose to receive:

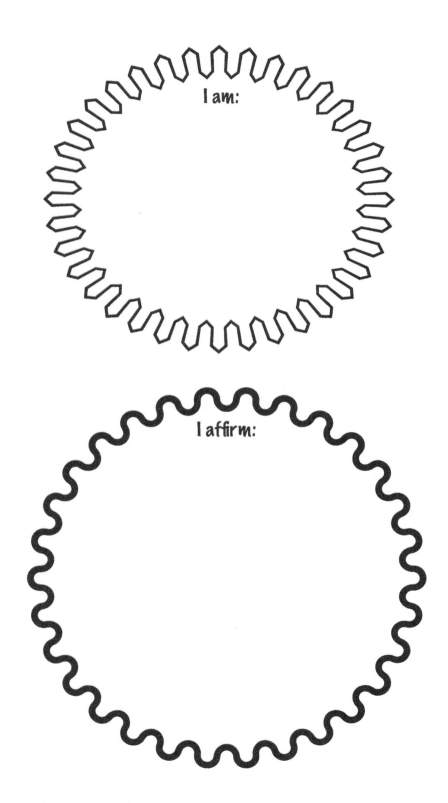

I am:

I affirm:

Notes

Notes

Made in the USA
Coppell, TX
15 May 2023

16901603R00066